WEST COUNTRY WARSHIPS
Royal Navy

Leo Marriott

**Air
Sea
Media**

First published 2014 by Air Sea Media Services, an imprint of Forty Editorial Services Ltd
www.airseamedia.co.uk

ISBN 978-0-9576915-1-3

Note on photographs

Unless otherwise stated, all the colour images in this book are in the copyright of the author, and monochrome images are authorised copies of originals from the US National Archives. Details of how to obtain original prints or digital image files of any of the photos in this book are given on our website www.airseamedia.co.uk

Glossary

AEFS	Ammunition, Explosives, Food, Stores (RFA)
ASW	Anti-submarine warfare
AUWE	Admiralty Underwater Weapons Establishment (Portland)
BRNC	Britannia Royal Naval College (Dartmouth)
CIWS	Close In Weapon System
FOST	Flag Officer Sea Training
FS	Frigate Squadron
HMC	Her Majesty's Cutter
HMCS	Her Majesty's Canadian Ship
HMS	Her Majesty's Ship
LCU	Landing craft utility
LCVP	Landing craft vehicle and personnel
LPD	Landing platform (dock)
LPH	Landing platform (helicopter)
LSD	Landing ship dock
LSL	Landing Ship (Logistic)
MARS	Marine Afloat Reach and Sustainability
MCMV	Mine countermeasures vessel
MEXE	Mechanical Engineering Experimental Establishment
MoD	Ministry of Defence
OPV	Offshore Patrol Vessel
RAF	Royal Air Force
RAS	Replenishment at sea
RFA	Royal Fleet Auxiliary
RM	Royal Marines
RMAS	Royal Maritime Auxiliary Service
RN	Royal Navy
SAM	Surface to air missile
SD	Serco Denholm
SDR	Strategic Defence Review
SSM	Surface to Surface Missile
SSN	Nuclear powered attack submarine
STOVL	Short Take Off, Vertical Landing
TA	Towed Array (passive sonar)

Pennant Numbers

Most warships and auxiliaries carry identifying letters and numbers on their hulls. In the NATO system the letter indicates the ship's function and each ship has an individual number. Letter codes applicable to RN ships are listed below.

A	Auxiliary Ship
D	Destroyer
F	Frigate
H	Survey vessel
L	Amphibious warfare vessel
M	Mine warfare vessel
P	Patrol craft
R	Aircraft Carrier
S	Submarine (pennant numbers not normally displayed)

PREVIOUS PAGE: An evocative scene as HMS *Illustrious* cruises at sunset off Rame Head.

RIGHT: Plymouth Sound forms a natural amphitheatre to observe naval movements and on most days there is something of interest to be seen such as HMS *Somerset*, a Type 23 frigate, shown here anchored off Jennycliff in the summer of 2013.

Contents

Introduction   4
1 The Modern Royal Navy   12
2 Hot and Cold Wars   38
3 1980s: The Falklands Decade   56
4 1990s: A Peace Dividend   82
5 A New Millennium   116
Index of Ships   143

OPPOSITE:
Plymouth and other
West Country ports
were heavily involved
in the build up for
Operation Overlord,
code name for the
D-Day Normandy
landings in June 1944.
Here US troops wait to
be ferried out to their
transports from the ferry
hard at Torpoint. In
the background are
numerous allied
warships. *ASM Archive*

INTRODUCTION

The West Country has a maritime heritage stretching back for centuries and has always been associated with the Royal Navy. This book highlights that connection through a collection of photographs, mostly taken by the author over the past 30 or 40 years, but also including some archive material to set the historic perspective. As the major naval port in the south-west, the emphasis is inevitably upon Plymouth and Devonport but other locations such as Falmouth, Dartmouth and Portland are not forgotten.

The port of Plymouth with its large natural harbour formed by the Sound and Cawsand Bay, together with sheltered anchorages in the Plym and Tamar estuaries, has long provided a base for naval operations. There is evidence of such activity as far back as Roman times but the city is probably best known for its association with Sir Francis Drake and the defeat of the Spanish Armada in 1588. Until that time, and for almost a century afterwards, the main anchorage used by both warships and merchant vessels was the Cattewater at the entrance to the River Plym. This gave access to Sutton harbour and was protected by gun batteries on both sides of the river.

It was not until the end of the 17th century that work began on the construction of a dockyard and naval base on the banks of the River Tamar to the west of Plymouth. As the sailing navy expanded and Britain was involved in a series of colonial wars throughout the 18th century, Plymouth rose in importance to rival the long established dockyards at Portsmouth and the Medway. As well as manning and fitting out ships for service around the world, Plymouth was in a strategically important location overseeing the approaches to the English Channel and providing a focal point for the fleets blockading the French coast during the Napoleonic wars.

In Victorian times the dockyard expanded northwards along the east bank of the River Tamar towards Keyham and the borough of Devonport which had grown up around the naval base took on the aspect of a major town. Other naval facilities at that time included the Naval Hospital and the Royal William Victualling Yard, both situated on Stonehouse Creek. In 1914, just before the outbreak of World War I, the boroughs of Devonport, Stonehouse and Plymouth were merged and were accorded city status in 1928.

Plymouth played an important role in both world wars and was associated with many famous actions. The battlecruisers *Invincible* and *Inflexible* sailed from here in November 1914 on their way to the Falklands where they destroyed a force of German cruisers under Vice Admiral Von Spee who had previously inflicted a crushing defeat on the Royal Navy at the battle of Coronel. In

World War II the West Country-manned cruiser HMS *Exeter* arrived to a tumultuous welcome early in 1940 after being extensively damaged in the battle of the River Plate. In 1944 Plymouth and the adjacent ports and harbours played a significant part in Operation Overlord, the Normandy Invasion.

In modern times the Plymouth has maintained its importance as a naval base: indeed, it is often cited as being the largest in Western Europe. In times of an ever-contracting navy, it has survived the closures which have occurred at Chatham and Rosyth.

Over the centuries the citizens of Plymouth have witnessed the passage of warships arriving or departing to perform their various duties. The nature of such ships has changed greatly. For centuries there were the stately wooden walls, the sailing ships-of-the-line, which were a constant reminder of Britain's global empire. These were followed in Victorian times by the early steamships which rapidly evolved into the massive Dreadnought battleships of World War I together with their attendant cruisers and destroyers, and the new and significant submarines and early aircraft carriers.

In World War II these were joined by a host of anti-submarine vessels and the variety of specialised ships and craft required for amphibious operations. Since then the appearance of warships, as well as their numbers, have changed considerably. Gone are the serried ranks of guns, replaced by missiles and electronic systems, while submarines are now nuclear-powered and can carry an awesome variety of weapons. In addition there are many

LEFT: The dockyard complex on the west bank of the River Tamar at Devonport is the centre of Royal Navy activity in the West Country. The section shown in this view was first developed in Victorian times as a major northward extension of the earlier dockyard dating from the 17th century.

BELOW: One of the Royal Navy's latest warships, the Type 45 destroyer HMS *Dragon*, presents a fine profile against a dramatic sky off Penlee Point.

support vessels without which the Royal Navy would be unable to operate. Many of these comprise the Royal Fleet Auxiliary Service but there are numerous dockyard craft which were once manned by the Royal Maritime Auxiliary Service but today are operated by various civilian contracting companies and in the process gradually losing their distinctive black and buff colouring.

Apart from Plymouth, the West Country's other location with a major current Royal Navy connection is the ancient town of Dartmouth—currently home to the Britannia Royal Navy College where the service's future officers are trained along with those of many overseas navies. Officer training was transferred to Dartmouth from Portland in 1863 but initially cadets were accommodated in the wooden hulk of HMS *Britannia*, from which the college takes its name, later joined by HMS *Hindustan*. The latter name is now borne by a decommissioned minehunter used as a static training vessel. The impressive college building complex dates from 1905 but seagoing training was provided by ships of the Dartmouth Training Squadron until the early 1970s since when cadets have been attached to regular ships on normal deployments. Today the only Royal Navy vessels regularly seen at Dartmouth are the pinnaces attached to the college but other warships often visit and there is nearly always one present during the annual Dartmouth Regatta held over the August Bank Holiday weekend.

At one time Portland harbour ranked with Plymouth as a naval base. Although lacking significant dockyard facilities, it offered an excellent protected anchorage and opened as a Naval base in 1845. The sheltered waters of Weymouth Bay were supplemented by massive breakwaters constructed between 1848 and 1905 which completely enclosed the anchorage. During World War I Portland was the base for the Royal Navy's Channel Fleet but for most of World War II it was too close to German bombers based in France to offer a secure harbour for the Home Fleet which remained at Scapa Flow in the Orkneys. After 1945 Portland was mainly home to various training units as well as vessels engaged on trial with the Admiralty Underwater Weapons Establishment. A notable activity was the working up of newly commissioned ships under auspices of Flag Officer Sea Training but this programme—together with the associated staff—was moved to Plymouth when Portland closed as a naval base in 1998.

Although never a naval base on the scale of Plymouth or Portland, the port of Falmouth nevertheless has played a significant role in naval history. Endowed with a natural deepwater harbour and occupying a strategically important point astride the entrance to the English channel, its history is littered with significant naval events. It was here in 1805 that the schooner HMS *Pickle* arrived bearing the first news of Nelson's spectacular victory at Trafalgar in 1805. In 1836 HMS *Beagle* anchored on its return from Charles Darwin's momentous survey voyage to the Pacific. Development of the modern docks dates from the mid-19th century and were heavily utilised for the

OPPOSITE: A once common sight in Plymouth Sound, HMS *Cornwall* was one of four Batch 3 Type 22 frigates which were based at Devonport until all were withdrawn from service in 2011 in the wake of the 2010 Strategic Defence Review and subsequently sold for scrapping.

INSET: Support for Plymouth's warships comes from a flotilla of dockyard craft which are a common sight around the port and include this tug now operated by the private contractor Serco Denholm on behalf of the MoD.

ABOVE: The RN makes frequent use of the facilities offered by the shipyards at Falmouth. Secured alongside in this photo is RFA *Argus* which is permanently based at the port.

repair of naval vessels in both world wars. During World War II a major costal forces base was set up at Mylor and in March 1942 the destroyer HMS *Camp-beltown* and a flotilla of small craft sailed from Falmouth on Operation Chariot, the famous raid to destroy the dock facilities at St. Nazaire and prevent their use by the German navy. Today the Royal Navy maintains a connection by the continued use of the docks refits and repairs and nominating Falmouth as the base port for the RFA *Argus* (casualty receiving and aviation training ship).

A significant proportion of the Royal Navy's warships and auxiliaries from around the time of the Falklands War (1982) right up to the present day are illustrated in this book, while a flavour of earlier times is presented in the Chapter 2. In addition there a a number of photographs showing vessels operated by MoD contractors as well as those belonging to other Government agencies such as HMRC who maintain a fleet of sophisticated patrol vessels. A companion volume covering the warships of visiting navies is currently in preparation.

OPPOSITE: Portland naval base closed in 1998 but some of the facilities are still used by civilian repair contractors. In the foreground is the former naval helicopter base (HMS *Osprey*) now the site of a major watersports facility which was venue for the sailing events in the 2012 Olympics.

LEFT: Dartmouth is home to the Britannia Royal Naval College where the service's future officers are trained. While the dedicated Dartmouth Training Squadron has long since been disbanded, RN warships are still regular visitors and the college's pinnaces are an everyday sight.

OPPOSITE: Pictured passing Millbay, HMS *Illustrious* is the only aircraft carrier remaining in the current fleet. Since the withdrawal of the Harrier force in 2010 she now operates as a helicopter carrier. Her sister ships *Invincible* and *Ark Royal* were decommissioned in 2005 and 2011 and scrapped.

INSET: Tugs assist *Illustrious* as she enters the Hamoaze for the dockyard at Devonport. *Illustrious* faces an uncertain future when she is withdrawn from service in 2014 and may be scrapped if no viable preservation scheme is in place.

For centuries the Royal Navy was the world's most powerful and at the start of the 20th century embraced the concept of a Two Power Standard, under which it would be equal in strength to any two other of the world's navies combined. The rapid rise of the German navy and events of the subsequent World War I made such an ideal unaffordable and the 1921 Washington Naval Treaty placed further restrictions on warship construction programmes. The Royal Navy was forced to accept parity (on paper at least) with the US Navy, although it was still numerically superior at the outbreak of World War II in 1939. However by 1945, even though it still possessed a massive fleet, it had ceded naval leadership to the United States and during the Cold War Era it also fell behind the Soviet Union which built up a large fleet of very heavily armed warships as well as a substantial submarine fleet. It was the latter which led the Royal Navy to invest heavily in ASW vessels with emphasis only changing with the thawing of East–West relations in the 1990s. In the meantime the unexpected Falklands War illustrated the need to be able to operate in the face of determined air opposition (nothing new there!) as well as the importance of amphibious warfare. Despite the pressure on an ever-decreasing defence budget, the Royal Navy maintained a balanced, if contracting fleet

until the infamous 2010 Strategic Defence Review which overnight took it out of the front rank of the world's navies. The last operational aircraft carrier, HMS *Ark Royal*, was withdrawn and the entire Harrier force was grounded and sold off. In addition the RAF maritime reconnaissance squadrons were disbanded and the replacement Nimrod MR.4 project cancelled, aircraft already produced being immediately broken up. The decommissioning of Type 42 destroyers and Type 22 frigates was accelerated so that today the Navy has only 13 Type 23 frigates and six new Type 45 destroyers (not all of the latter are yet available for operational duty).

Looking forward there are some bright spots. Two massive new aircraft carriers are under construction with the lead ship HMS *Queen Elizabeth II* due to commission in 2016 and her sister ship, HMS *Prince of Wales*, to follow in 2018. On paper these will carry an air group consisting of 36 Lockheed Martin F-35B Lightning II STOVL fighters, six Merlin ASW helicopters and four AEW helicopters (yet to be ordered). In practice it is highly unlikely that the full air group would ever be embarked and given that the flight deck arrangements are designed for STOVL operations it will not be possible to operate other combat aircraft such as the French Rafale or the US Navy's F/A-18

OPPOSITE: The Type 45 destroyers are the most modern ships in the current fleet. The first of a class of six was HMS *Daring* (D32) which commissioned in 2009 and is shown here alongside at Devonport. Their main armament is the Aster SAM. They are carried in the vertical launch silo situated on the fore-deck.

RIGHT: At anchor in Plymouth Sound is HMS *Argyll* (pennant number F231), one of seven Type 23 'Duke' class frigates which form a major element of the Royal Navy's Devonport Flotilla. The remaining six Type 23s are based at Portsmouth

Hornet. In fact it is still not certain that both carriers will remain with the Royal Navy, there being political pressure to sell off one of them. Even if both are retained, only one is likely to be in commission at any given time.

The rest of the surface fleet will comprise the 19 Type 45 destroyers and Type 23 frigates although the latter will be gradually replaced (hopefully at least on a one for one basis) from 2020 onwards by the new Type 26 frigate. By comparision, at the time of the Falklands War the Navy had two carriers in commission (*Invincible* and *Hermes*) and two more nearing completion as well as 15 missile-armed destroyers and

over 40 frigates as well as others under construction. Admittedly not all of these were in commission but the comparison with today's fleet clearly illustrates the continued run down of the fleet.

The nuclear-powered submarine fleet is also contracting and by 2022 it will consist only of the seven 'Astute' class (although it must be admitted that these are highly capable world class submarines) and the four existing 'Vanguard' class carrying the UK's nuclear deterrent in the form of the Trident SLBM.

Looked at from a West Country point of view, Plymouth is still a major naval base but is not as busy as Portsmouth in terms of the ships based here. The new

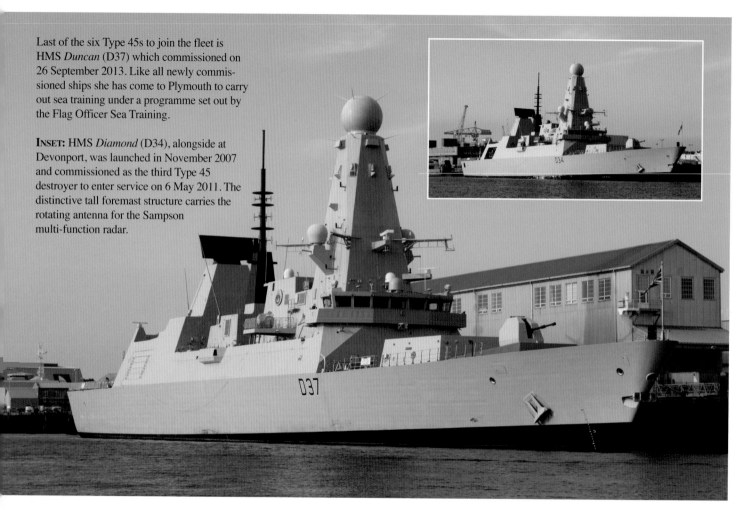

Last of the six Type 45s to join the fleet is HMS *Duncan* (D37) which commissioned on 26 September 2013. Like all newly commissioned ships she has come to Plymouth to carry out sea training under a programme set out by the Flag Officer Sea Training.

INSET: HMS *Diamond* (D34), alongside at Devonport, was launched in November 2007 and commissioned as the third Type 45 destroyer to enter service on 6 May 2011. The distinctive tall foremast structure carries the rotating antenna for the Sampson multi-function radar.

aircraft carriers and all of the Type 45 destroyers are based at Portsmouth while the Type 23 fleet is split between the two ports. Plymouth's Devonport dockyard also has facilities for the repair and maintenance of nuclear-powered submarines and all of the existing 'Trafalgar' class boats are based here, presumably to be followed by the new 'Astute' class as the older boats are withdrawn.

A major role of the naval base is to act as a head-quarters and centre for the Royal Marines and amphibious warfare vessels. This element of the Royal Navy as fared relatively well in recent years, partly as a result of lessons learnt in the Falklands as well as the nature of littoral operations since then. The assault ships *Albion* and *Bulwark* are based here as well as the helicopter carrier HMS *Ocean*, the latter currently the largest surface warship in the fleet, although she will be dwarfed by the new carriers when they enter service. In support of amphibious operations are the three 'Bay' class LSDs which are a common sight in Plymouth Sound (a fourth vessel of this class was sold to Australia). A new facility which brings together all elements of the Royal Marine assault forces in the Plymouth area has been created on the north side of Weston Mill lake. Officially titled RM Tamar it is now the base for all the small landing and assault craft (including LCAC hovercraft) was well as the major amphibious warships (i.e. *Ocean*, *Albion*, *Bulwark*)

Devonport is also home to the Royal Navy's fleet of hydrographic survey vessels which consist of the 13,500-ton HMS *Scott* and the much smaller 3,500-ton HMS *Echo* and HMS *Enterprise*. Smallest of all is the coastal survey ship HMS *Gleaner* which at 26 tons is the Navy's smallest commissioned ship.

The photographs in this section were almost all taken in the 12 months prior to publication and comprise examples of those ships of the modern Royal Navy which are likely to be seen today in West Country waters.

LEFT AND BELOW: Built by Swan Hunter at Wallsend on Tyne, the appropriately named HMS *Northumberland* (F238) was launched on 4 April 1992 and commissioned on 29 November 1994. Current plans call for the 13 'Duke' class to be progressively replaced by the new Type 26 frigates due to enter service from 2020 onwards but *Northumberland* is scheduled to remain in service until 2029. In the photo below, *Northumberland* prepares to anchor in Plymouth Sound. The Type 23 was designed predominately as an ASW frigate and just visible in the stern gallery is the yellow body of the Type 2037 active sonar which at sea is deployed at the end of a long towed array which in turn functions as a passive sonar.

BELOW: Normally based at Portsmouth but shown here silhouetted against the morning light in Plymouth Sound, HMS *St. Albans* (F83) was the last of 16 Type 23 frigates. Built by Yarrow Shipbuilders, Glasgow, she was launched on 6 May 2000 and commissioned on 6 June 2002.

RIGHT: HMS *Portland* (F79) is one of the youngest Type 23s having commissioned in May 2001. At the time of writing (November 2013) *Portland* was commanded by Commander Sarah West, the first woman to command a major Royal Navy warship.

ABOVE: Ships that pass. HMS *Northumberland* (F238) enters Plymouth Sound as her sister ship HMS *Kent* (F78), a Portsmouth-based Type 23, is heading out to sea.

Devonport is the base
for the Royal Navy's
amphibious warfare
vessels.

OPPOSITE, ABOVE:
Largest is the 22,000-
ton helicopter carrier
HMS *Ocean* (L12),
here anchored outside
the breakwater.

OPPOSITE, BELOW:
Bulwark's sister ship is
HMS *Albion* (L14).
Note the stern gate
which can be lowered to
allow landing craft to
enter.

LEFT: HMS *Bulwark*
(L15) is one of two
LPDs. Designed to
carry some 700 troops
and their vehicles and
equipment, it has
a floodable stern dock
housing assault craft
and a flight deck
above it.

BELOW: This aerial view of HMS *Sutherland* (F81) off the Cornish coast clearly shows the layout of these ships. Most of the armament including the automatic 4.5in gun, Seawolf missile silo and Harpoon missile containers (not fitted in this case) are grouped forward of the bridge leaving the after section devoted to the hangar and flight deck.

OPPOSITE, INSET LEFT: The two assault ships (see pages 22–23) are backed up by three 'Bay' class LSDs, which also have a floodable stern dock and a helicopter landing deck. However they lack many of the facilities of the assault ships and are operated as civilian manned Royal Fleet Auxiliaries. Shown here is RFA *Mounts Bay* (L3008) moored in Plymouth Sound.

OPPOSITE, INSET RIGHT: RFA *Lyme Bay* (L3007) in the sound with the fleet tanker RFA *Orangeleaf* moored astern. The design of the 'Bay' class is such that most of the crew and troop accommodation is in the massive superstructure block leaving hull space fee for vehicle stowage. Up to 24 62-ton Challenger tanks can be stowed.

RIGHT: Each of the LPDs can accommodate four LCU Mk 10 landing craft of the type shown here which can carry one of the Army's Challenger tanks or several smaller vehicles or 120 troops. They are fitted with interlocking bow and stern ramps so as to facilitate loading in the crowded confines of the LPD dock.

INSET: Incidents involving anti-nuclear protestors and other activist groups, as well as potential terrorist threats, mean that any of the nuclear-powered submarines entering or leaving Devonport and the sound are closely escorted by tugs and other MoD craft. Here HMS *Talent* is hardly visible sandwiched between the Serco Denholm tugs *Adept* and *Forceful*.

RIGHT: The 'Trafalgar' class boats are covered with acoustic tiles intended to absorb sonar transmissions, making them harder to be detected and tracked. After extended periods at sea these tend to break away as illustrated here.

INSET: The dockyard at Devonport has extensive facilities for the maintenance and refitting of nuclear-powered submarines and is home to the remaining five 'Trafalgar' class SSNs. Originally a class of seven boats, *Trafalgar* and *Turbulent* were decommissioned in 2009 and 2001 respectively. Shown here leaving the Hamoaze is HMS *Talent* (S92) which originally commissioned in May 1990.

RIGHT: HMS *Tyne* (P281), pictured at Falmouth Docks, is one of three 'River' class ocean patrol vessels employed almost exclusively on fishery protection duties. A fourth vessel built to a modified design, HMS *Clyde* (P257), is assigned as the Falklands Islands guardship.

BELOW RIGHT: The RN has always placed great emphasis on accurate hydrographic surveying and the resulting Admiralty charts are used world-wide. They also monitor sea conditions such as temperature, salinity and currents. The largest of the Devonport-based survey vessels is the 13,500-ton HMS *Scott* (H131).

LEFT: HMS *Biter* (P270) is one of a fleet of 16 'P2000' class small patrol craft operated by the Royal Navy. Most form the First Patrol Boat Squadron and are allocated to University Royal Navy Units where they provide maritime and naval experience to undergraduates. Commissioned in 1986 *Biter* is allocated to Manchester and Salford Universities.

LEFT AND OPPOSITE: A colourful recent addition to the fleet is the Devonport-based ice patrol vessel HMS *Protector* (A173), since 2011 chartered as a replacement for HMS *Endurance* which was seriously damaged in a flooding incident off Chile in 2008. In September 2013 it was announced that she had been purchased from her Norwegian owners and that *Endurance* will be sold off. *Protector* has a bluff icebreaker bow, an enclosed crow's nest for lookouts to monitor ice conditions ahead, a powerful crane amidships and a large helicopter deck covers the stern. The funnel carries an appropriate penguin motif.

OPPOSITE: Moored in the sound, the 31,500-ton RFA *Wave Ruler* (A390) is one of two large fleet tankers which entered service in 2003 and are equipped for underway RAS. The overhanging stern carries a large flight deck and a hangar capable of housing a Merlin helicopter is built into the superstructure.

LEFT: Alongside on the Rubble Jetty at Devonport, the small fleet tanker RFA *Gold Rover* is one of the oldest ships in the fleet having entered service in 1974. Originally a class of five ships, only two remain in service (the other is RAF *Black River*) and are a common sight in the West Country.

RIGHT: Many of the tasks previously carried out by the Royal Maritime Auxiliary Service have now been contracted out to private companies of which the most significant is Serco Denholm Marine Services. Their largest vessel is the newly built SD *Victoria*, a 2,500-ton multipurpose research and support vessel which replaced the previous SD *Newton* in 2010. Since this photo was taken the ship has been repainted in SD house colours with white upperworks and funnels.

LEFT: RFA *Orangeleaf* is the sole survivor of a class of four commercial tankers taken over for military use and commissioned between 1979 and 1984. Intended originally for the bulk transport of oil fuel, they were subsequently fitted with RAS gear so as to be able support ships at sea. Photo shows *Orangeleaf* anchored off Plymouth.

RIGHT: Traditionally RMAS vessels had black hulls and buff upperworks and funnels but since being taken over by Serco Denholm a company livery is gradually being introduced. Originally the only change was that funnels were painted red but but now a livery of white upperworks and funnels is being applied. The state of change in the summer of 2013 is illustrated by these SD tugs (*Careful* and *Faithful*), one of which is only partially repainted.

LEFT: Another MOD contractor is Smit International which operates a fleet of fast Range Safety Vessels and Aircrew Training Vessels at various UK locations. Amongst the latter is the *Smit Dee* seen passing the Plymouth Breakwater. The design includes a clear after deck for helicopter winching operations and these vessels can also carry out torpedo recovery and other general tasks.

2 HOT AND COLD WARS

This chapter is illustrated by images of a variety of Royal Navy warships which were to be seen at Plymouth from during and after World War II up to the 1970s. During the war the dockyard was constantly occupied with the repair and refit of damaged ships and was itself in the frontline as an obvious target for Luftwaffe bombers based in France. Indeed the city and dockyard suffered heavily in the 1941 blitz and and subsequent raids. From an operational point of view it saw a constant stream of escort vessels involved in the battle of the Atlantic and its destroyer flotillas were constantly in action harrying German naval forces based at various French ports. In particular, the 10th Destroyer Flotilla—comprising mainly the heavily armed 'Tribal' class destroyers—fought several fierce engagements with German forces in the English Channel before and after Operation Overlord, the D-Day landings on 6 June 1944. In the lead up to Overlord and subsequently in support of allied forces ashore, such operations became increasingly important.

Virtually every West Country port was involved in the build up to Overlord. The US forces which would land on Utah and Omaha beaches in Normandy were all stationed in the West Country and South Wales. Two divisions of the US V Corps embarked at Weymouth and Portland; two more divisions of the US VII Corps embarked at Devon ports including Torquay, Brixham, Dartmouth and Plymouth; the 29th US Division embarked at various points around Falmouth. In addition a large area of coastal land at Slapton Sands was requisitioned for training by US forces in amphibious warfare techniques.

After World War II the Royal Navy was inevitably run down and dozens of ships were scrapped or laid up in reserve. Many of the latter were rafted up in moorings along the upper reaches of the Hamoaze and River Tamer where they remained a common sight until the late 1950s when this assembly of increasingly obsolete ships was finally dispersed and sold off. However, the run down of naval strength was halted by two factors the first of which was the onset of the so-called Cold War and the threat posed from around 1950 onwards by the substantial increase in the size of the Russian submarine fleet. This led to many of the laid-up destroyers being put back into service after conversion to fast anti-submarine frigates, much of the necessary work being done at Devonport dockyard. The other factor was the outbreak of the Korean War which again resulted in ships being taken out of reserve and—after a hasty refit—being dispatched to the Far East until the end of active hostilities in 1953.

LEFT: The 'Tribal' class destroyer HMS *Tartar* (wartime pennant number G43) at anchor in Plymouth Sound in the spring of 1944. At this time she was leader of the Plymouth-based 10th Destroyer Flotilla which was engaged in a number of fierce actions against German coastal forces in the lead up to D-Day.

BELOW RIGHT:
Plymouth was a major
embarkation port for
US forces taking part
in Operation Overlord.
These LSTs are load-
ing troops of the US
4th Infantry Division
at the Mount Edge-
cumbe shore adjoining
Barne Pool, today a
popular anchorage for
yachts.

OPPOSITE: Today the
River Dart throngs
with ferries and
pleasure craft but in
1944 it was a different
story. Rows of landing
craft and tank landing
ships prepare for
Operation Overlord
while a screen of
barrage balloons,
intended to deter low
flying aircraft, flies
overhead.

By the end of the 1950s the RN was undergoing a major technological revolution with guided missiles replacing guns and the use of gas turbines for propulsion was being investigated. In addition, the ending of national service in the early 1960s led the RN to improve living conditions aboard warships in order to assist the recruiting and retention of volunteer sailors. These changes demanded new types of warships such as the 'County' class guided-missile destroyers and a whole range of new and specialised frigates, all of which were to be seen at Plymouth and off the West Country coast. The main role of the RN was now to act in concert with other NATO navies to nullify the Russian submarine threat—a role which became increasingly important as nuclear-powered ballistic missile-carrying submarines began to enter service in the early 1960s.

However, despite the construction of new ships the RN continued to shrink in size as a result of a continuing series of cuts to the nation's defence budget and it was not only ship numbers which were being reduced. For decades after the war the RN maintained major dockyards at Plymouth, Portsmouth, Chatham and Rosyth as well as major establishments at other ports such as Portland, Pembroke and Londonderry. Inevitably as the size of the fleet reduced

HMS *Devonshire* was a 'County' class heavy
cruiser completed in 1929 and was actually
built at Devonport dockyard. After arduous
war service she was converted to a cadet
training ship in 1947 and all armament except
for the forward 8in gun turret was removed.

these bases could not all be sustained and, despite its size and importance, there were several occasions when the future of the Devonport dockyard and Naval Base was was seriously in doubt. Once again the decline of the Royal Navy was halted by a war when Argentine forces invaded the Falkland Islands, 8,000 miles away in the South Atlantic. The dockyard played a major part in preparing ships at short notice for the Falklands campaign and the entire Devonport-based 4th Frigate Squadron made up of the 'Amazon' class Type 21 frigates was dispatched to the South Atlantic where they made up a major element of the task force and were heavily involved in the fighting, sadly losing two ships in the process.

This chapter reviews the various types of warships which would have been seen around Plymouth and the West Country coast from World War II up until the time of the Falklands War in 1982.

BELOW LEFT: Pictured in the sound in 1960, HMS *Lion* (C34) was one of a class of three light cruisers under construction at the end of World War II which were initially laid up before eventually being completed to a revised design incorporating a main armament of four automatic 6in guns. *Lion* commissioned in 1960 but had a short operational life, being laid up in 1965 although her sister ships (*Tiger* and *Blake*) were converted to carry helicopters and served until the end of the 1970s.

ABOVE: HMS *Broadsword*, shown passing Mount Edgecumbe park c.1960, was one of a class of 16 'Weapon' class destroyers ordered in 1943 but with the end of hostilities most of these were cancelled and only four were completed as fast fleet escorts. *Broadsword* was later converted to an aircraft direction ship by the addition of a long range radar on a lattice mast just forward of the funnel. Laid up in 1963, she was scrapped in 1968.

RIGHT: Proceeding up the Hamoaze in 1962, HMS *Venus* (F50) was a wartime destroyer commissioned in 1943 but in 1952–54 she was converted to a Type 15 fast anti-submarine frigate at Devonport dockyard. For a few years before being decommissioned in 1963 she served with the 17th Frigate Squadron which acted as the training squadron for cadets from the BRNC Dartmouth.

RIGHT: Anchored in the River Dart is the 'Whitby' class Type 12 frigate HMS *Eastbourne* (F73) while serving with the Dartmouth Training Squadron in the 1960s. The 15 'Whitby' and 'Rothesay' class, together with a total of 26 Type 12 (Modified) 'Leander' class frigates, formed the backbone of the Royal Navy's ASW force from the late 1950s until well after the Falklands War in 1982.

Portland Navy Days 1975 and an SRN5 Hovercraft is put through its paces. The Inter-Service Hovercraft Trials Unit (IHTU) was established at Lee-on-Solent in 1974 and evaluated several different types until disbanded in 1982. More modern types are now in service with the assault ships *Albion* and *Bulwark*. In the background is the Type 21 frigate HMS *Ambuscade* (F172)

ABOVE: The Type 21 frigate HMS *Antelope* (F170) alongside at Devonport in August 1979. Like most of her sister ships, she was deployed to the Falklands in April 1982 but on 22 May she was hit by a bomb while supporting the San Carlos landings. The bomb did not explode on impact but it did go off later while attempts were being made to defuse it killing one of the army engineers and wounding others, although the ship's crew had already been evacuated. The explosion wrecked the ship which later sank, one of two Type 21s lost in the campaign (the other being HMS *Ardent*).

RIGHT: Even in the late 1970s a number of World War II veterans could be seen in the upper reaches of the Hamoaze. HMS *Forth* entered service in 1939 as a submarine depot ship and in the 1960s was modernised to support nuclear submarines, acting as the parent ship for the Devonport based 2nd Submarine Flotilla. Between 1972 and 1978 she formed part of the shore establishment HMS *Defiance* until the new Fleet Maintenance Base opened in 1978 when she was then laid up awaiting disposal.

Another veteran was LST3043 *Messina*, a tank landing ship completed in 1945. In 1957 she was one of the support vessels for Operation Grapple, the British A-bomb tests on Christmas Island. During the 1960s she served in the Gulf area before ending up as store hulk at Devonport in 1969. This photo was taken in 1979 and she was scrapped in the following year.

INSET: Shown laid up in 1979, HMS *Salisbury* was one of a class of four Type 61 aircraft direction frigates built in the 1950s. She was decommissioned in 1978 and was to have been sold to Egypt but this deal fell through and she returned to Devonport to act as a static sea training ship for HMS *Raleigh*, the naval training establishment at Torpoint, until finally expended as a target in 1985.

LEFT: The 1970s marked the rundown of the RN's fixed-wing carrier fleet and HMS *Eagle* was laid up opposite Millbrook Creek 1972–78 when she was towed away for scrapping. In her place came HMS *Ark Royal*, shown here in 1979 before going to meet a similar fate in the following year.

ABOVE RIGHT:
No fewer than 26 'Leander' class frigates were built for the Royal Navy between 1959 and 1973. The original armament included a twin 4.5in gun on the foredeck but by 1980 when this photo of HMS *Naiad* (F39) alongside at Devonport was taken, the original ten Batch I ships had been converted to specialist ASW vessels and the torpedo-carrying Ikara anti-submarine missile and launcher system replaced the guns.

LEFT: In the 1970s the eight Type 21 frigates were based at Devonport as the 4th Frigate Squadron. In contrast to other contemporary RN warships which were built to Admiralty designs based on Naval Staff requirements, the Type 21s were designed and built by a private company, Vosper Thorneycroft. The result was particularly handsome warship whose clean lines are shown as HMS *Alacrity* (F174) heads across the sound.

ABOVE: Intended as a successor to the 'Leander' class, the Type 22 'Broadsword' class frigates were considerably larger and were the first major RN warships to dispense with the gun as part of the main armament. Instead, they carried Seawolf missile launchers fore and aft for defence against air attack—a combination which proved to be extremely effective in the Falklands. Shown here at Devonport in the summer of 1981 are the first two Type 22s, HMS *Battleaxe* (F89) with HMS *Broadsword* (F88) inboard.

LEFT: Despite a steady contraction in the size of the RN, the 1970s saw a considerable investment in the infrastructure of the dockyard at Devonport. In addition to the new Fleet Maintenance Base at the northern end, the other major project was the enormous Frigate Complex at the south end, which comprised three covered dry docks together with all services and facilities. Opened in 1977, this impressive structure now dominates the riverside skyline. *Devonport Dockyard Press Office.*

RIGHT: By 1980 when this photo was taken the RN had a dozen nuclear-powered attack submarines but still maintained a fleet of around a dozen 'Oberon' and 'Porpoise' diesel-electric submarines. Although lacking the range, speed and endurance of their nuclear counterparts, they still offered a unique combination of qualities and were noted as being particularly quiet (and therefore difficult to detect and track). Shown here is an 'Oberon' class boat undergoing a refit in drydock at Devonport.

LEFT: The ocean going tug RMAS *Roysterer* (A361) was an everyday sight at Devonport during the 1970s and 80s but was later transferred to the Clyde. One of a class of three launched in 1970, she was listed for disposal in 1995.

BELOW: The events of April 1982 imposed a considerable extra workload on the dockyard at Devonport. Apart from warships, a lot of effort was put into modifying and converting ships taken up from the trade (STUFT). One important project was adapting the container ship Atlantic Conveyer to transport Chinook helicopters and Sea Harrier STOVL jet fighters to the Falklands. In the event the ship was hit by an Exocet missile on 25 May and subsequently sank. Although the Harriers had already flown off, all but one of the vital helicopters were lost. *BAE Systems*

3 1980s: THE FALKLANDS DECADE

OPPOSITE: The Type 21 frigate HMS *Active* (F171) passes Mount Wise in the summer of 1983 on passage up-river to Devonport. She was the fifth of the class to join the fleet and the last of three to be built at Vosper Thornycroft's Southampton yard (the rest being built on the Clyde by Yarrow Shipbuilders), commissioning in June 1977. Like her sister ships she was involved in the Falklands, sailing from the UK on 10 May 1982 and later provided gun support for the assault on Tumbledown Mount, the last major action of the land campaign.

In the aftermath of the Falklands the RN was held in high regard by the British public and many politicians. The immediate benefits were that planned reductions in strength were halted and several new warships were ordered. In 1981 the then Defence Secretary, John Nott, had proposed a substantial reduction in the Royal Navy's surface fleet including the sale of the carrier *Invincible* to Australia but in the wake of the Falklands War this was all put aside. Regrettably the Royal Navy lost four warships during the campaign— the Type 42 destroyers *Sheffield* and *Coventry*, and the Type 21 frigates *Antelope* and *Ardent*. However, in December 1982 the government announced that no fewer than five new Type 22 frigates would be ordered as direct replacements and others were subsequently ordered bringing the total to 14 ships of this class. In the light of the Falklands experience the last four (Batch III) were redesigned to carry a 4.5in automatic gun which considerably increased their effectiveness. The Type 22s were organised into three frigate squadrons of which the first four Batch I ships formed the 2nd FS, the six long-hulled Batch II formed the 1st FS, while the four Batch III were designated as the 8th FS.

The six remaining Type 21 frigates of the 4th Frigate Squadron remained in service and were a common sight at Plymouth and off the West Country coast. They were not retired until 1993–94 when they were all sold to Pakistan and are still in commission today (2013). The once substantial numbers of 'Leander' class frigates were gradually run down from 1988 onwards and one of the last to go was HMS *Scylla* which decommissioned in December 1993. This ship had several West Country connections, the most significant being that she was the last major warship built at Devonport dockyard having been launched on 8 August 1968. After being laid up for several years she was eventually towed out and sunk in Whitsand Bay to form an artificial reef which today is a major attraction for divers.

Devonport continued as the base for the nuclear powered attack submarines the six 'Swiftsure' class boats being joined by the first of the improved 'Trafalgar' class. At the same time the first generation nuclear-powered boats, including HMS *Conquerer* which had sunk the Argentine cruiser *Belgrano* during the Falklands War, began to be retired. This was the start of a problem which even today has not be satisfactorily resolved in that the decommissioned nuclear-powered submarines could not be broken up and scrapped in the normal way due to the hazardous nature of their nuclear reactors. Consequently they and successive decommissioned boats are moored in

BELOW RIGHT: HMS *Arrow* (F173) undergoing maintenance alongside the Devonport Frigate Complex. The Type 21s were the first major warships designed from the outset to be powered solely by gas turbines, in this case two 25,000shp Rolls-Royce Olympus and two 4250shp RM1A Tyne gas turbines. The ship could make 18 knots cruising on the two Tynes and maximum speed was 32 knots with all units operating.

the dockyard's No.3 Basin awaiting a long-term solution to the disposal of the nuclear materials.

Apart from the nuclear boats the RN also maintained a force of conventional diesel-electric submarines. At the start of the decade this comprised 13 'Oberon' class as well as few of the older 'Porpoise' class. By the end of the decade this had reduced to

less than a dozen although the new 'Upholder' class were in prospect.

In this chapter is a selection of photographs showing the many and varied RN ships to be seen in Plymouth waters during the 1980s although the emphasis is inevitably on the various classes of frigates which were such common sights in those days but have now gone.

HMS *Ambuscade* (F172) passing Millbay docks. The first three Type 21s including *Ambuscade* were not fitted with Exocet missile launchers forward of the bridge when completed and they had still not been installed when this photo was taken in August 1983.

Home for Christmas! HMS Avenger (F185) prepares to go alongside at Devonport assisted by tugs in December 1985. After several years arduous service, including periods in the inhospitable South Atlantic the hulls of several Type 21s showed signs of strain. Measures taken to strengthen the hull included a metal beam riveted to the hull amidships which can be seen this view of the ship.

ABOVE RIGHT: In the 1980s 'Leander' class frigates were still the most numerous in the fleet. Shown passing Cremyll village, HMS *Cleopatra* (F28) was modernised in 1975 when Exocet launchers replaced the twin 4.5in turret and a second Seacat SAM system was installed on the hangar roof. The large winch on the stern is associated with the towed array of a passive sonar. These ships were designated Batch 2(TA) 'Leanders'.

RIGHT: HMS *Alacrity* (F174) anchored in Plymouth Sound, November 1985. With sister ships *Antelope* and *Arrow* she was one of the first Type 21s to reach the Falklands, sailing with the main task group. She saw considerable action, sinking an Argentine supply vessel, being attacked from the air on at least ten occasions, and was escorting the *Atlantic Conveyer* when it was hit and set on fire by an Exocet missile.

INSET, LEFT: A rust-streaked HMS *Penelope* (F127) alongside at Devonport during a much needed maintenance period, August 1983. During the 1970s this ship acted as a trials vessel for the development of the Seawolf missile system. Subsequently she was refitted as a Batch 2 Exocet-armed 'Leander', this work being carried out at Devonport and completed in March 1981.

INSET, RIGHT: HMS *Galatea* was a Batch 1 'Leander' class frigate which was converted to an Ikara-armed ASW frigate at Devonport in 1973–74. In the immediate post-Falklands era many distinguishing features such as the black funnel cap and coloured ships boats were overpainted in a uniform grey. In addition pennant numbers were also deleted but later restored as illustrated in this 1983 photo.

RIGHT: The last ten 'Leanders' had a modified hull with slightly increased beam. Subsequently they were to be modernised by replacing the Seacat missile system with the much more effective Seawolf but only five ships were eventually so modified between 1980 and 1984. One of these was HMS *Hermione* (F58), here being moved by tugs after her modernisation refit at Devonport in the summer of 1983.

LEFT: The 'Leander' class frigates were developed from the 'Whitby/Rothesay' class Type 12 frigates of which the last and most well known was HMS *Plymouth* (F126) which is shown off Plymouth Hoe flying her decommissioning pennant on 28 April 1988. Built at Devonport and launched in July 1959, she was in the thick of the Falklands War and remained in action despite several bomb hits and near misses. *RN Photo*

RIGHT: Almost as soon as she was taken out of service, HMS *Plymouth* was handed over to the Warship Preservation Trust and in the summer of 1988 was berthed in Millbay Docks where she was open to the public. However, a permanent berth was not available and the ship has moved several times ending up at Birkenhead. Since the trust went into administration in 2006, the condition of the ships has deteriorated and so far efforts to find a berth in its Plymouth home have been unsuccessful and it is more than likely that she will eventually be scrapped. A sad fate for an historic fighting ship.

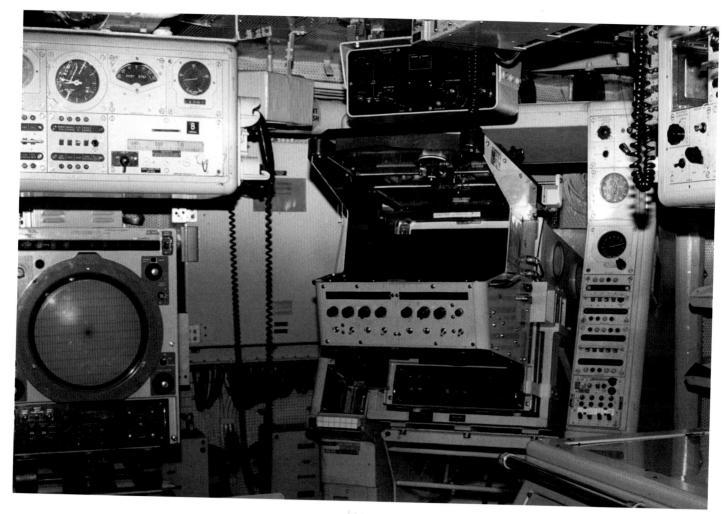

LEFT: Visitors to HMS *Plymouth* in 1988 had access to all parts of the ship including the operations room shown here. The cramped layout and orange-tinted radar screens contrast with the more spacious compartments with banks of computerised displays in modern warships.

RIGHT: An increasingly common sight in the 1980s were the Type 22 missile-armed frigates. 14 were completed between 1979 and 1990, two of which are shown alongside at Devonport in August 1988. The inboard ship is HMS *Brave* (F94) and the other is HMS *Boxer* (F92), both serving at that time with the 1st Frigate Squadron. Both were Batch 2 ships which featured a lengthened hull.

RIGHT: The length of the original Batch 1 Type 22 frigate design was constrained by the size of the covered drydocks in the Devonport Frigate Complex. Even so it was a tight fit as is demonstrated by the first of the class, HMS *Broadsword* (F88). Lack of space to accommodate modern weapons systems and electronic equipment led to the enlarged Batch 2 ships in which the hull was lengthened by 55 feet (16.76m). *Devonport Dockyard Press Office*

OPPOSITE: With the Type 22 frigates the Royal Navy appeared to be going back to the traditional alphabetic class names for flotilla vessels—the A of the 'Amazon' class Type 21 now being followed by the B of the Type 22s. However, the eighth Type 22 broke this progression when it was named HMS *London* (F95) as a result of a request from that city's mayor and council. The next two ships were named *Sheffield* and *Coventry* in memory of destroyers lost in the Falklands. London is shown alongside at Devonport shortly after commissioning in June 1987.

RIGHT: Present at the 1989 Navy Days was the minehunter HMS *Brecon* (M29), the name ship of a class of 13 ships which entered service 1980–89. They were the first major warships designed from the outset to be constructed of reinforced glassfibre mouldings which, apart from advantages in cost and ease of construction, also significantly reduced the magnetic signature.

BELOW LEFT: The last four Type 22 frigates (Batch 3) were completed to an upgraded design utilising experience gained in the Falklands. Apart from the obvious addition of an automatic 4.5in gun, other changes included the replacement of Exocet SSMs by the more capable Harpoon and new efficient Rolls-Royce Spey gas turbines which almost doubled the ships' endurance. First of the new Batch 3 ships was HMS *Cornwall* (F99) which commissioned in 1988.

BELOW: Dressed overall, the newly commissioned Batch 3 Type 22 frigate HMS *Campbeltown* (F86) was the star attraction at Plymouth's 1989 Navy Days. Ships open to the public included two other Type 22s (*London* and *Brilliant*), four Type 21s and three 'Leander' class—an impressive line up which could not be repeated today.

RIGHT: In the 1950s the RN commissioned no fewer than 118 'Ton' class coastal minesweepers which were widely used for patrol and training duties. By the end of the 1980s only around a dozen remained including HMS *Stubbington* (M1204) pictured here in Plymouth Sound. Commissioned in 1954, she was sold and broken up in 1992.

BELOW LEFT: Off Plymouth in August 1983, HMS *Guernsey* (P297) was one of a class of seven offshore patrol vessels built in the 1970s. They were used almost exclusively on fishery protection duties as indicated by the blue and yellow pennant symbol attached to the funnel. All seven were built by Hall Russell & Co Ltd at their Aberdeen shipyard and the trawler influence on the design is obvious.

BELOW: During the 1980s the Royal Navy continued to maintain a substantial fleet of ocean going survey vessels with their distinctive white hulls and buff funnels. HMS *Hecla* (A133), here moored alongside 2 Jetty in Devonport's south yard, was the nameship of a class of three similar vessels which originally commissioned in 1965–66.

BELOW: In 1989 when this photo was taken the 2nd Submarine Squadron at Devonport comprised no less than eleven nuclear powered hunter killer submarines, five 'Swiftsure' class and six of the newer 'Trafalgar' class. Outboard is HMS *Superb* (S109) with a sister boat inboard. Commissioned in 1976 she was retired in 2008 after damage incurred in a grounding incident in the Red Sea.

RIGHT: HMS *Swiftsure* (S126), name ship of her class, in Plymouth Sound (August 1988). Built by Vickers Shipbuilding at Barrow-in-Furness and completed in 1973, her service career was prematurely ended in 1992 when her pressure hull was seriously damaged during trials.

BELOW: RFA *Sir Geraint* was one of six logistic landing ships (LSLs) built in the 1960s and named after various knights of King Arthur's Round Table. Despite being civilian-manned fleet auxiliaries, all six formed an essential part of the Falklands Task Force in 1982, and sister ship *Sir Galahad* was lost and three other suffered varying degrees of damage in heavy air attacks. However, *Sir Geraint* bore a charmed life and was undamaged. Shown here at Devonport in 1985, she was sold off in 2005.

RIGHT: The fleet replenishment ship RFA *Regent* (A486) moored in the Hamoaze, June 1984. Along with her sister ship *Resource*, she commissioned in 1967 and they were the first vessels designed for the role which had previously been carried out by converted merchant ships. They acted as a 'one stop shop' for warships at sea, providing ammunition, explosives, food and stores as well as a limited amount of fuel oil. Note the helicopter flight deck and hangar atop the after superstructure.

ABOVE RIGHT: To support worldwide fleet activities a substantial number of civilian-manned RFA tankers were required. Amongst the most capable of these in the 1980s were the three 'OL' class of which RFA *Olmeda* (A124) is shown entering Plymouth in the summer of 1987. The several derricks and hoses are part of the RAS gear which enable oil fuel to be transferred to other ships whilst both are underway. Commissioned in 1965, she was originally named *Oleander* but this was later changed to avoid confusion with the frigate *Leander*.

RIGHT: Supplementing the two 'Resource' class were the two newer and slightly larger 23,600-ton 'Fort' class which entered service in 1978–79. Shown alongside at Devonport is RFA *Fort Austin* (A386). In addition to their normal fleet support duties, these ships had the capacity to embark and support operations by up to four Sea King ASW helicopters supplying AS protection for a task group.

The RFA *Appleleaf* (A79) was originally ordered and launched as the civilian *Hudson Deep* in 1975 but together with a sister ship (RFA *Brambleleaf*, ex-*Hudson Cavalier*) was taken over by the MoD when the order was cancelled. They were modified for use as fleet tankers and although their main role was the bulk transfer of oil stores they were equipped with RAS gear to enable them to act as support tankers when required. Here assisted by RMAS tugs, *Appleleaf* passes Drake's Island in August 1989.

The tug RMAS *Saluki* stands by as the Type 21 frigate HMS *Avenger* berths at Devonport in 1985. Saluki was one of a class of 19 harbour tugs built between 1962 and 1972. Taken over by Serco Denholm in 2008, she was sold to a West African buyer in 2010 after almost 40 years' service.

Proceeding up the Hamoaze to the Armament Depot at Ernesettle is the armaments carrier RMAS *Kinterbury* (A378). Built at the north Devon shipyard at Appledore and completed in 1980 she was one of a class of three ships used for transporting stores including shells, missiles, torpedoes and depth charges between the various naval bases. She was sold off in 2005.

OPPOSITE: The three
'Invincible' class
aircraft carriers were in
service throughout this
decade but, being
based at Portsmouth,
were relatively infre-
quent visitors to
Plymouth. In this
instance HMS *Ark
Royal* (R07), dressed
overall for the occa-
sion, forms the main
attraction at the 1991
Devonport Navy Days.
Commissioned in
1985, she was the last
of the class to enter
service.

4 1990s: A PEACE DIVIDEND

The fall of the Berlin Wall in November 1989 was one incident in a chain of events which led to dissolution of the Soviet Union in December 1991. It effectively marked the end of the Cold War between eastern and western ideologies which had existed from the time of the Berlin blockade in 1948. For over 40 years the size and shape of the Royal Navy had been organised around the potential threat of the military forces of the Soviet bloc, particularly their massive submarine fleet which included many armed with nuclear ballistic missiles. Suddenly in a new age of Glasnost, this raison d'etre was gone and a reappraisal was necessary. In the 1980s the RN had not done too badly with several new ships joining the fleet to more than make up for the losses in the Falklands. However, it was inevitable in the 1990s that questions would be asked about the necessity to maintain the armed forces, including the navy, at their Cold War levels and it was not long before a desire for a 'Peace Dividend' coupled with financial necessity brought about a series of defence reviews which in the following decade substantially reduced the size of the RN.

In 1990 the navy had around 50 destroyers and frigates available, although not all were in commission. This figure included over a dozen 'Leander' class frigates which were nearing the end of their useful lives but on the plus side the new Type 23 frigates were just coming into service (eventually 16 of these would be built). However, it was not long before this figure was drastically reduced as a result a defence review entitled 'Options for Change'. All six of the Type 21 frigates were sold to Pakistan in 1993–94 followed by the four Batch 1 Type 22s to Brazil in a deal negotiated in 1994 while all the remaining Leanders had been decommissioned by the end of 1993. So by the end of the decade there were only around 30 destroyers and frigates with only a handful of new ships projected. A similar state of affairs affected submarine numbers where all conventional diesel-electric submarines had been decommissioned, including four brand new 'Upholder' class boats which were eventually sold to Canada, leaving an all-nuclear fleet. Numbers of mine warfare vessels were also substantially reduced and there was a corresponding reduction in the auxiliary vessels needed to support the fleet.

On a brighter note the three 'Invincible' carriers were still available and the new helicopter carrier HMS *Ocean* had entered service. In addition two new assault ships, *Albion* and *Bulwark*, were under construction and would replace the long serving HMS *Fearless* (HMS *Intrepid* had been decommissioned in 1999 after a long period in reserve). This reflected the increased

importance given to amphibious operations in what was previously considered 'out of area' operations

Despite the reduction in strength following the end of the Cold War, the Royal Navy was busier than ever. It was closely involved in the Gulf War in 1990–91 and in a notable event a Sea Dart missile fired from the Type 42 destroyer HMS *Gloucester* intercepted an Iraqi Silkworm missile which was about to hit the American battleship USS *Missouri*. After the war significant RN assets remained in the Gulf to support forces ashore and also to clear and make safe a considerable number of mines. Other actions later in the decade included acting in support of NATO and UN actions in the independent states set up following the break up of the former Yugoslavia.

As far as the West Country was concerned a major event in this period was the closure in 1998 of the Portland Naval Base where Flag Officer Sea Training had been based. This organisation then moved to Plymouth, where some elements of FOST had already begun operating a few years earlier, and this helped to make up for the loss of the many frigates. Ships such as the Type 42 destroyers became more common visitors, quite apart from a regular influx of warships from various NATO and other navies which will form the material for a forthcoming companion volume depicting the many foreign naval visitors.

In the meantime the varying fortunes of the Royal Navy in the post Cold War Era are illustrated by the images on the following pages in this chapter.

A busy scene in Plymouth Sound during April 1999. In the foreground is the carrier HMS *Illustrious* taking on supplies from small craft alongside. In the background is the aviation training ship RFA *Argus* (A135).

RIGHT: RFA *Argus*, pictured in 1999, was originally completed as a container ship in 1981 as the *Contender Bezant* but was temporarily requisitioned as a support ship during the Falklands War. Returned to her civilian owners she was subsequently purchased by the MoD and converted to an aviation training ship, commissioning in 1988 when she replaced the smaller but purpose built RFA *Engadine*. When not engaged in the training of helicopter pilots, she has an alternative role as as a primary casualty receiving ship having been equipped with the necessary hospital facilities.

INSET: By the early 1990s the few survivors of the once numerous 'Leander' class frigates were approaching the end of their operational lives with the Royal Navy. The Batch 2 conversion HMS *Danae* (F47) is shown entering Devonport in July 1991. Later that year she was sold to Ecuador and renamed Moran Valverde, serving on until 2008, 43 years after being launched at Devonport in 1965.

LEFT AND INSET: HMS *Active* (F171) underway off the Cornish coast, August 1991. She was transferred to Pakistan on 23 September 1994 and renamed *Shah Jahan*. All six ex-RN Type 21s remain in service today with the Pakistan Navy but their Exocet missiles have been replaced by the more modern Harpoon SSM and the Seacat short range SAM by the Chinese LY 60N missile system.

ABOVE: The rakish-looking Type 21 frigates also came to the end of their RN careers in the 1990s The six survivors (two were sunk in the Falklands) were sold to Pakistan in a package deal signed in 1993. Seen leaving Devonport in August 1992, HMS *Amazon* (F169) was later transferred to the Pakistan Navy on 30 September 1993 and renamed *Babur*.

RIGHT: HMS *Brilliant* (F90) was one of the original four short-hulled Batch 1 Type 22 frigates and commissioned in 1981. Despite being relatively modern these ships were not immune to various defence cuts and all four were sold to Brazil in a deal signed in November 1994, although *Brilliant* was not transferred until 31 August 1996 when she was formally renamed Dodsworth (after Jorge Dodsworth Martins, a Brazilian Admiral in World War II who subsequently became Minister of Marine in 1946)

ABOVE: A dramatic shot of the Type 22 frigate *Battleaxe* (F89) lit up at night while acting as the traditional guard ship for the Dartmouth Regatta in August 1993. *Battleaxe* was the last of the four Type 22s to be transferred to Brazil, on 30 April 1997, and was renamed *Rademaker* (after a Brazilian Admiral who became the country's Vice-President in 1969)

RIGHT AND INSET: Almost invariably the Red Arrows perform at the annual Dartmouth Regatta and in this case their exciting display is centred over HMS *Battleaxe* moored in the River Dart opposite the town. There can be few more spectacular venues for the Arrow's Hawks to perform their routine.

RIGHT: The six Batch 2 Type 22 frigates were built to a modified design which featured a lengthened hull and a larger hangar so that the ship could operate the new Merlin ASW helicopter then coming into service. The last pair were ordered in the wake of the Falklands War and were named *Sheffield* and *Coventry* in memory of the two Type 42 destroyers lost during the campaign. This view of HMS *Sheffield* (F96) heading down the River Tamar in 1996 clearly illustrates the longer hull and sharply raked bow.

INSET: A stern view of HMS *Coventry* (F98) in 1997 shows the enlarged hangar and flight-deck incorporated into the Batch 2 vessels. As the size of the fleet was progressively reduced following the end of the Cold War, *Coventry* was decommissioned in 2001 after only 13 years service and was subsequently sold to Romania along with sister ship HMS *London* (HMS *Sheffield* was decommissioned in 2002 and sold to Chile)

BELOW: HMS *Campbeltown* (F86) commissioned in May 1989. Shown dressed overall in May 1995, she was one of several RN vessels taking part in events at Plymouth to commemorate the 50th anniversary of VE-Day, the end of World War II in Europe.

INSET RGHT: As the older frigates were scrapped or sold off, their place was taken by the new Type 23 'Duke' class frigate although the rate of commissioning was not enough to prevent a decline if the strength of the surface fleet. Designed in the Cold War era, they were optimised as ASW platforms although still packing a punch with a 4.5in gun and Harpoon SSMs, as well as vertically launched Seawolf SAMs. The first Type 23 was HMS *Norfolk* (F230) which commissioned in November 1989 and is shown at Devonport in July 1991.

BELOW: Mounting a 4.5in automatic gun, a Goalkeeper CIWS, Seawolf SAM and Harpoon SSM, the 5,250-ton Batch 3 Type 22 frigates were the most heavily armed surface ships in the fleet and were retained in service until the notorious Strategic Defence Review in 2010 led to their decommissioning. Shown crossing Plymouth Sound in better times is HMS *Cornwall* (F99) which was the first of the Batch 3 vessels to commission (in 1988).

ABOVE: The last four Type 42s (Batch 3) featured a lengthened bow to improve seaworthiness and this is clearly shown in the 1999 view of HMS *Edinburgh* (D97). The main armament of the Type 42 was the Sea Dart surface-to-air missile system which provided long range air defence for a task force and proved very effective in the Falklands. In total 12 Type 42s were commissioned between 1973 and 1985 and although two were lost in the Falklands, they continued to provide the fleet's air defence for almost another three decades.

RIGHT: HMS *Argyll* (F231) was the second Type 23 to enter service and commissioned in May 1991. Here she is moored in front of Plymouth Hoe during the VE-Day 50th anniversary commemoration in 1995. The Type 23s were the first British warships in which the anti-aircraft missiles (Seawolf) were contained in a vertical lunch silo, an arrangement which dispensed with the complexity of trainable launchers as the missiles were programmed to turn onto the required target bearing immediately after launch.

BELOW: With Devonport specialising in supporting the various frigate squadrons, the Portsmouth-based Type 42 destroyers were a less common sight in the West Country. However, when FOST moved from Portland to Plymouth in the mid-1990s they became more frequent visitors. Anchored in the sound in the summer of 1997 is HMS *Nottingham* (D91) which commissioned in 1983. She was one of four Batch 2 ships which featured an improved main search radar and weapon control system compared to the original six Batch 1 ships.

RIGHT: One of the lessons learnt in the Falklands War was the need for a fully automatic Close In Weapons System (CIWS) to combat low-flying aircraft such as the A4 Skyhawks which sank HMS *Coventry* and incoming missiles such as the Exocet which sank HMS *Sheffield*. The remaining Type 42 destroyers were subsequently equipped with the American Phalanx system which incorporated a rapid-firing 30mm Vulcan cannon. This shows one installed aboard HMS *Nottingham*.

LEFT: Up to the mid-1990s the Royal Navy continued to operate conventional diesel-electric submarines of which the 'Oberon' class was the most numerous, 13 being built for the RN between 1959 and 1967. They were extremely successful boats and were particularly quiet when running underwater. This unidentified example passing Mount Wise in the summer of 1990 shows the remains of a camouflage scheme on her hull, indicating that she had at sometime been engaged on a covert mission.

BELOW: The planned successor to the 'Oberon' class was the 'Upholder' class of which four were ordered during the 1980s. Shown here is the lead boat, HMS/M *Upholder* which commissioned in December 1989. The design was based on the Vickers Type 2400 and incorporated a very sophisticated sonar suite while the main armament comprised six bow-mounted 21in tubes for Tigerfish wire-guided torpedoes.

BELOW: With the older 'Oberon' class scrapped and the 'Upholder' class prematurely laid up in 1994, the Royal Navy now had an all nuclear powered submarine force made up of five 'Swiftsure' and seven 'Trafalgar' class attack submarines (plus the four 'Vanguard' class strategic missile submarines). HMS *Talent* here crossing Plymouth Sound in 1994, was the sixth of the class to enter service and commissioned on 12 May 1990.

RIGHT: A close-up of the conning tower of HMS *Ursula* as she passes the Type 22 frigate HMS *Beaver* at Devonport in June 1994. Despite being brand new all four 'Upholder' class were decommissioned laid up at the end of that year as part of a programme of substantial defence cuts. Subsequently they were sold to Canada in 1998 (*Ursula* became HMCS *Corner Brook* while *Upholder* became HMCS *Chiquotimi*) and all four remain in service today.

RIGHT: Even in the post-Cold War period it was apparent that British forces could be called on to act at short notice in response to international events. Consequently the Navy's Amphibious Warfare Squadron was less affected by the series of defence cuts in the 1990s. From the mid-1960s the backbone of this was the two assault ships HMS *Fearless* and *Intrepid*, both of which played a major part in the San Carlos landings during the Falklands War. Moored inside the Plymouth breakwater is HMS *Fearless* (L10) in 1999 nearing the end of her operational life (she was paid off in 2002, the Royal Navy's last steam-powered warship).

Fearless and *Intrepid* were classified as LPD (landing platform dock) as the after section of the ship incorporated a dock for landing and assault craft. Here one of the ship's four 16-ton LCVPs passes in front of HMS *Fearless*. These small assault craft were carried on davits while four of the larger LCUs could be accommodated in the dock.

LEFT AND INSET: The 20,500-ton HMS *Ocean* (L12) was the Royal Navy's first purpose-built helicopter carrier, previous examples all being converted fixed wing carriers. Classified as LPH (landing platform—helicopter) she is shown at Devonport in the summer of 1999 less than a year after commissioning on 30 September 1998. In addition to helicopters, she also could carry four LCVPs. HMS *Ocean* was designed to support an air group of up to 12 Sea King HC.4 helicopters, two of which are shown parked on the flight deck in this inset view. Subsequently these have been replaced with the larger Merlin HC.3. The ship is capable of carrying and landing a Royal Marine Commando (approximately 600–800 troops) and most of their vehicles and equipment.

ABOVE: The large assault ships were backed up by the smaller LSLs (landing ships, logistic) of the 'Sir Lancelot' class which are operated as civilian-manned Royal Fleet Auxiliaries. Originally a class of six completed in the 1960s, RFA *Sir Galahad* was lost in the Falklands and RFA *Sir Tristram* (L3505) was badly damaged. However, the latter ship was repaired and the opportunity taken to lengthen the hull and enlarge the flightdeck to allow operation of Chinook helicopters. Photo shows her at Plymouth in 1995

INSET ABOVE: A new LSL was ordered to replace the lost *Sir Galahad*. Built by Swan Hunters on the Tyne, the new ship was launched on 13 December 1986 and took the name of her predecessor. The new RFA *Sir Galahad* (L3005) is here in Plymouth Sound in 1995 and is carrying a set of pontoons known as MEXE floats affixed to the hull sides. These can be detached and used for a variety of purposes such as making a connecting roadway from the bow doors to a beach, or even as dumb lighters or barges for landing supplies.

BLACK ROVER

A273

OPPOSITE: Alongside at Devonport (1996) is RFA *Black Rover* (A273), one of a class of five small but extremely useful fleet tankers. She commissioned on 23 August 1974 and remains in service today.

LEFT: RFA *Fort Grange* (A385) underway off the Cornish coast during a FOST exercise in 1995. Clearly seen in this view is the spacious flightdeck and large hangar which allowed a detachment of four Sea King helicopters to be embarked.

LEFT: Towards the end of the 1990s the Royal Navy's survey vessels abandoned their traditional white hulls and buff funnels and adopted a standard warship grey. This is illustrated by this view HMS *Roebuck* (H130) in Cawsand Bay in the summer of 1999. *Roebuck* was one of the newest survey vessels being completed in 1986 and had a secondary role as a an MCM support ship.

INSET LEFT: The ocean-going survey vessel HMS *Hecla* (A133) turns in the River Tamar in 1995, only two years before she was laid up after a career spanning 32 years. During the Falklands War she acted as an ambulance ship, carrying casualties out to the hospital ship SS *Uganda* stationed safely outside the range of Argentine aircraft.

BELOW: 'Hunt' class minehunter HMS *Dulverton* (M35) heads out from Devonport on a clear and sunny October day, 1994. The 13 'Hunt' class ships were the most sophisticated of the Navy's MCM forces and they and the expertise of their crews were in constant demand, particularly during and after the two Gulf wars.

INSET LEFT: Twelve 'River' class minesweepers were commissioned in the 1980s and were intended to be manned by the RNR. However four were sold to Bangladesh in 1994 and three to Brazil in 1995. Illustrated at Devonport in 1996 is HMS *Orwell* (M2011) which at that time was acting as a training ship for BRNC Dartmouth.

LEFT: Visiting Dartmouth in the summer of 1990 is the 'Isles' class offshore patrol vessel HMS *Anglesey* (P277). At this time there were seven such vessels in service forming the Offshore Division of the Fishery Protection Squadron.

RIGHT: Repair and maintenance of the MoD's many auxiliary craft provided work for many South West boatyards. On the slipway at Polruan on the River Fowey is the 'Clovelly' class fleet tender RMAS *Headcorn* (A1766), one a large number of such vessels which performed numerous and varied duties around the UK. At this time (1994) *Headcorn* was based at Falmouth and supported helicopter activities from nearby RNAS Culdrose.

The last of the three 'Invincible' class to operate as a strike carrier with Sea Harriers embarked was HMS *Ark Royal* (R07) shown here in Plymouth Sound (September 2002) with the RFA *Fort Victoria* in the background. This fine ship was unexpectedly withdrawn from service in 2010 and subsequently scrapped leaving the RN without organic fixed-wing capability. Sister ship HMS *Illustrious*, although still in service operates only as a helicopter carrier.

5 A NEW MILLENNIUM

The Royal Navy entered the new millennium still contracting in the wake of the end of the Cold War and a never ending round of defence cuts. By the end of the first decade it was reduced to one operational aircraft carrier and 23 destroyers and frigates, and even these numbers were further reduced by the 2010 Defence Review (SDR) which axed the carrier HMS *Ark Royal* and her Harrier jets as well as scheduling the remaining four Type 22 frigates for decommissioning. Nevertheless there were some bright spots. In particular, amphibious warfare forces had done well with the helicopter carrier HMS *Ocean*, which had commissioned in 1998, being joined by two purpose-designed 18,000-ton assault ships (HMS *Albion* and HMS *Bulwark* which commissioned in 2003). In addition four new 'Bay' class Landing Ship (Dock) entered service in 2006–07, although one of these was subsequently sold to Australia as a result of the SDR. As well as these major warships, a new fleet of specialised landing craft was procured to operate from them. With Plymouth now the major base for the Royal Marines and associated Army units, these ships are regularly berthed at Devonport and are often seen anchored in the Sound.

By the year 2000 the air defence of the fleet rested mainly on the Type 42 destroyers, of which 11 were available although their numbers were gradually run down with the last four Batch III vessels decommissioned between 2011 and 2013. Their intended replacement was the new Type 45 destroyer of which the lead ship, HMS *Daring*, commissioned in 2009. Originally it was hoped that these would replace the older ships on a one for one basis with 12 to be ordered. However, this unsurprisingly proved to be unrealistic and the number was reduced to eight and then to six, all of which are now in service. Although the Type 45s are based at Portsmouth, they are regularly seen in West Country waters as they carry out pre-deployment training with FOST.

The Type 22 frigates had been a familiar sight at Plymouth from 1979 when the first of class (HMS *Broadsword*) commissioned but in the first decade of the new millennium their numbers rapidly diminished. The four Batch I ships had already been sold to Brazil and by 2004 three Batch II ships had been scrapped or sunk as targets and the other three sold to Chile and Romania. This left the only four Batch III ships which—despite their undoubted qualities—were all scheduled for disposal in the wake of the 2010 SDR. Even the smaller Type 23 frigates did not escape, three relatively young ships of this class being sold to Chile following the 2004 Defence Review, the remaining 13 now being the only frigates in service with the Royal Navy. Although due to

BELOW RIGHT: At the start of the 21st century the RN still retained all three aircraft carriers and the lead ship, HMS *Invincible* (R05), is shown in the sound in July 2003. However, two years later she was decommissioned and laid up, subsequently being sold in 2011 and towed to Turkey for scrapping. A further blow to naval aviation was the withdrawal of the specialised air defence Sea Harrier F/A.2 in 2004 leaving only the GR.7/9 ground-attack variant available for deployment aboard the carriers.

be replaced by the new Type 26 global combat ship, delays with this project have led to the service life of the Type 23s being extended until as late as 2036. In a perverse way this is good news for Devonport Dockyard as considerable maintenance and refit work will be required to keep these ships going.

A similar story applies to the Devonport-based nuclear submarines. By 2010 all of the 'Swiftsure' class had been withdrawn and only six 'Trafalgar' class remained although the first of the new highly capable

'Astute' class had been completed. Although it was hoped that at least eight 'Astutes' would be ordered, it now seems likely that the final total will be only seven and, at the moment, it would appear that these will be based, at least initially, at Faslane in Scotland. Whether they will become a common sight at Plymouth remains to be seen.

The most significant project for the Royal Navy in recent years has been the highly contentious project to build two large aircraft carriers. The contract to

An atmospheric shot on a summer's evening off Plymouth in 2008. In the foreground is the helicopter carrier HMS *Ocean* (L12) with HMS *Illustrious* (R06) behind. Aboard the latter a noticeable feature is the third mast at the after end of the superstructure which was added at during a refit completed in 2007. At the same time she was modified to provide troop accommodation so that she could be used as an LPH — now her current role.

The helicopter carrier HMS *Ocean* represented a substantial boost to the Royal Navy's amphibious warfare forces when she entered service in 1998 and has had a busy operational career since then. This photo was taken in 2002 but less than 12 months later she was heading for the Persian Gulf as part of the British contribution to Operation Telic, the 2003 Iraq War. Noticeable in this view are the three Phalanx CIWS mountings, two at the stern and one on the bow, and a rear admiral's flag at the masthead.

build these two 66,000-ton vessels, the largest British warships ever, was formally agreed in 2008 but unfortunately various political and economic factors have conspired to reduce their effectiveness even before they enter service. The whole rationale for large carriers is that they can embark more aircraft and the large flight deck allows for conventional catapulted take offs and arrested landings. Although the new 'Queen Elizabeth' class vessels are designed to carry an air wing of in excess of 40 aircraft, it is highly unlikely that as many would ever be available in practice and the final decision to buy the F-35B VSTOL version of the Joint Strike Fighter (Lockheed Martin Lightning II) means that the vast flight deck will be under-utilised. Whatever the pros and cons of the carrier programme, it is undeniable that the cost of building and equipping these ships has had a significant effect on the naval budget, other projects such as the Type 45 destroyer being cut back as a result. Due to their size they will not be able to use the dockyard facilities at Devonport and even entering the anchorage in Plymouth Sound would be problematic, so it is unlikely that there will be many opportunities to view them in West Country waters.

BELOW LEFT: Substantial additions to the Royal Navy were the two new Assault ships, HMS *Albion* (L14) and HMS *Bulwark* (L15), which commissioned in 2003 and 2005 respectively. A feature of these ships was the large helicopter deck aft below which was a floodable dock which could accommodate four large landing craft (LCU) while four smaller LCVP were carried on davits amidships. This aerial view shows the ship dressed overall on the occasion of a fleet review held in Plymouth Sound in 2003 when HM The Queen presented Colours to the Royal Navy in a ceremony held aboard HMS *Ocean*.

HMS *Bulwark* (L15) commissioned in
April 2005 and is shown entering
Plymouth escorted by tugs in June
2007. Both assault ships are permanently based at Plymouth and can often
be seen secured alongside in Weston
Mill Lake where the RM Tamar base is
also situated.

INSET: Additional support capacity for amphibious operations is provided by the 'Bay' class auxiliary LSDs of which four entered service in 2006–07, replacing the long-serving 'Sir Lancelot' class LSLs. This is the newly completed RFA *Mounts Bay* (L3008) at anchor in Plymouth Sound in April 2006. Her sister ship *Largs Bay* was sold to Australia where she now serves as HMAS *Choules*.

RIGHT: Each of the assault ships can accommodate four 240-ton LCU Mk.10 which were specifically designed to operate from the new ships. Each can carry a Challenger tank, several smaller vehicles or up to 120 troops. The identifying code A4 on the side of the hull indicates that this is one of the four LCUs from HMS *Albion*. All landing craft are now painted in a disruptive camouflage scheme for deployment in the littoral environment.

ABOVE: Although based at Portsmouth, the 'Daring' class destroyers have been regular visitors to Plymouth as they carry out operational training with the FOST team. This stern quarter view of HMS *Dragon* (D35) off Plymouth in the summer of 2012 emphasises the angular stealth shape of the these ships. *Dragon* commissioned on 20 April 2012 and the sixth and last Type 45, HMS *Duncan*, on 26 September 2013.

RIGHT: The most significant additions to the fleet in recent years are the new air defence 'Daring' class Type 45 destroyers. Originally these were to have replaced the 12 long-serving Type 42s on a one for one basis but successive reviews saw this number cut to eight and then to six. First to enter service was HMS *Daring* (D32) which commissioned on 23 July 2009 and is shown anchored Cawsand Bay in June of the following year.

ABOVE: As part of the gradual rundown in naval strength all of the Batch 1 and 2 Type 22 class frigates had been withdrawn from service by 2002 with several subsequently being sold to foreign navies. The four Batch 2 ships continued to form a vital element of the Royal Navy's surface fleet and the announcement in the 2010 SDR that they would all be withdrawn in 2011 caused considerable concern, reducing the number of destroyers and frigates to an all time low of 19 vessels. Here HMS *Chatham* (F87) heels over as she takes the sharp turn in the channel off Devil's Point, Plymouth, in 2007.

ABOVE RIGHT: HMS *Liverpool* (D92) was the last of the short-hull Type 42 destroyers to be decommissioned. Having provided invaluable gunfire support during Operation Unified Protector off Libya in 2011, she was finally retired in March 2013 after a 32-year career with the Royal Navy. This view of the ship at Plymouth dates from 2000 at which time there were still ten Type 42 destroyers in service.

RIGHT: Being the newest ships, the four long-hulled Batch III Type 42 destroyers were the last to be phased out of service. HMS *Gloucester* (D96) is shown at Plymouth in 2008 and decommissioned along with HMS *Manchester* in 2011. HMS *York* followed in 2012 and HMS *Edinburgh* was the last to go in 2013.

The Type 23 was designed to accommodate the new Agusta Westland AW101 Merlin HM.1 anti-submarine helicopter which was substantially larger and heavier than the Sea King which it replaced from 2000 onwards. Here HMS *Monmouth* (F235) recovers her Merlin as she proceeds upriver at Devonport, August 2006. *Monmouth* commissioned in September 1993 and is scheduled to remain in service until 2027

RIGHT: At the start of the new millennium, the Type 23 'Duke' class frigates formed the most numerous RN class with 16 commissioned between 1990 and 2002. However, following the 2004 defence review, three of these (*Norfolk*, *Marlborough* and *Grafton*) were laid up and subsequently sold to Chile. HMS *Grafton* (F80) is photographed here dressed overall during the 2003 Plymouth Fleet Review.

RIGHT: A 'Trafalgar' class nuclear-powered submarine underway off Rame Head in 2003. At that time five 'Swiftsure' class boats also remained in commission although *Splendid* paid off later that year and the remaining four followed at intervals up 2010. The first of the 'Trafalgar' class was retired in 2008 and currently only five remain operational, although two of the new 'Astute' class have joined the fleet and are based at Faslane, Scotland.

BELOW: 'Duke' class frigate HMS *Iron Duke* (F234) passing Mount Wise on a glorious June day in 2006. A point of interest is that the ship has the new Mod.1 mounting for the 4.5in automatic gun with its distinctive angular shape for stealth purposes. At this time this mounting was progressively replacing the original egg-shaped Mod.0 mounting which had equipped RN frigates and destroyers from the 1970s. The name *Iron Duke* of course refers to the famous Duke of Wellington, victor of the Battle of Waterloo

RIGHT: 'Hunt' class MCMV HMS *Ledbury* (M30) underway in Plymouth Sound, July 2006. The 2004 defence review scheduled three 'Hunt' class to be decommissioned leaving only eight in service. Ledbury was built by Vosper Thornycroft at their Southampton yard, commissioned in June 1981, and today is based at Portsmouth with the 2nd Mine Countermeasures Squadron (MCMS).

ABOVE: HMS *Brecon* (M29) was the lead ship of the 'Hunt' class MCMVs and commissioned in 1980 but was laid up in 2005. Subsequently, in 2008 she was modified to act as a static training ship attached to HMS Raleigh, the Royal Navy's shore establishment at Torpoint in Cornwall where naval ratings undergo initial training. The ship is now permanently moored off Jupiter Point on the River Lynher, a tributary of the River Tamar.

ABOVE: A relatively rare sight in West Country waters are the 'Sandown' class single-role minehunters (SRMH). These are not equipped for conventional minesweeping but locate mines by means of sophisticated sonar systems and then destroy them with remote control mine disposal systems (RCMDS). Normally based at Faslane with the 1st MCMS, HMS *Walney* (M104) is shown at Plymouth in 2006 but she was laid up in 2010 leaving only seven out of an original class of twelve vessels still in service today.

RIGHT: The smallest commissioned vessel in the RN is the 26-ton inshore survey vessel HMS *Gleaner* (H86). Technically she is styled Her Majesty's Survey Motor Launch (HMSML) and is employed on regular port surveys around the UK. Built in 1983 she was due to retire in 2007 but after a refit is now expected to reamin in service until around 2018.

INSET: Two 3,500-ton 'Echo' class oceanic and hydrographic survey vessels were commissioned in 2003. They were built at Appledore Shipyards in North Devon under sub-contract to Vosper Thornycroft (now BAE Systems) who remain responsible for maintenance and repair under a 25-year agreement with the MoD. As with other survey vessels, they have a secondary role supporting MCM operations. This is HMS *Echo* (H87) pictured in 2007.

New additions to the fleet in 2003–04 were three 'River' class offshore patrol vessels which then replaced the older 'Isles' class. Shown here at Plymouth in August 2003 is the newly commissioned HMS *Severn* (P282), the other two being named *Tyne* and *Mersey*. These vessels are unusual in that they are not owned by the Navy but are leased from the builders, Vosper Thornycroft (now part of BAE Systems), who are contracted to make them available for at least 300 days each year.

RIGHT: BRNC Dartmouth has a fleet of eight 'P1000' class twin-screw picket boats used for training naval officer cadets. Built in the 1970s, they are a common sight on the River Dart and out in Start Bay. 40 years old, they are likely to be replaced when funding is available.

OPPOSITE: The Royal Navy currently has 16 'P2000' class patrol boats, most of which are allocated to the various University Royal Navy Units whose activities are co-ordinated by the Commodore BRNC. HMS *Tracker* (P274) shown at Dartmouth in 2008 is allocated to the Oxford University unit. She is one of two (the other is *Raider*) which are fitted with more powerful MTU diesels boosting max speed from 20 to 24 knots.

BELOW: One of the oddest-looking vessels in the fleet is the RFA *Diligence* (A132) which was originally built in Sweden as the *Stena Inspector* for North Sea oil support operations. Chartered in 1982 to act as a forward repair ship for the Falklands Task Force she was purchased in October 1983 and underwent substantial modifications to better suit her for the role. Carrying heay engineering equipment, the full-size helicopter deck constructed above the bridge superstructure is responsible for the ship's bizarre appearance.

INSET: Helicopters are a vital tool in RAS operations at sea. A Sea King HC.4 helicopter is here shown exercising with the RFA *Wave Knight* in 2003. Although the HC.4 remains in service today it is due to be replaced by modified Merlin troop-carrying helicopters transferred from the RAF.

RIGHT: The new large fleet tankers RFA *Wave Knight* and RFA *Wave Ruler* replaced the old tankers *Olwen* and *Olna* when they entered service in 2003. This aerial view shows RFA *Wave Knight* (A389) when participating in the 2003 fleet review in Plymouth Sound having just commissioned a few weeks earlier on 8 April. A feature of these two ships compared to older vessels is their double hull construction which helps to prevent oil spillage in the event of an accidental grounding. This feature is now mandatory on similar vessels being built today including the MARS tankers being built in South Korea for the Royal Navy.

RIGHT: The support tanker RFA *Orangeleaf* (A110) is the sole survivor of the original trio which were purchased from a commercial operator in the 1980s but is due to be retired in 2015. Her single-hull construction does not meet modern requirements.

INSET: Among the various vessels acting as tenders to carry personnel between Devonport and ships operating in the Plymouth area are the unusual 'Storm' class catamaran-hulled tenders SD *Cawsand* (A192) and SD *Bovisand*. A feature of the design is the Small Waterline Area Twin Hull (SWATH) configuration which is intended to give a smoother ride through rough seas. Both vessels act in support of FOST and are a daily sight in the sound.

ABOVE LEFT: *Fort Victoria* (A387), anchored at Plymouth i 2002, was one of a pair of large 32,000-ton fleet replenishment ships which entered service in 1993–94 and were intended to supplement the two 'Fort Grange' class which dated back to the late 1970s. These are extremely capable ships with four RAS rigs and facilities for up to five helicopters. However, sister ship *Fort George* was withdrawn from service in 2011 under the provisions of the SDR and *Fort Victoria* will follow in 2019, leaving the older *Fort Austin* and *Fort Rosalie* to soldier on until around 2022 by which time they will be over 40 years old.

LEFT: The commissioning of the new RFA *Fort George* in 1994 gave rise to the possibility of confusion with the existing *Fort Grange* (A385). Consequently in 2000 the latter was renamed *Fort Rosalie* (one of the 19th century forts around the Portsmouth Naval Base) and is shown in this guise alongside at Devonport in 2002.

INDEX OF SHIPS

ABOVE: A common sight in West Country waters are the fleet of vessels operated by Maritime Branch of the UK Border Agency which comprises four Damen 42m patrol craft. A fifth vessel was HMC *Sentinel*, a Vosper Thornycroft 37m design shown here at Plymouth in 2009, which was commissioned in 1993 but was retired in July 2013.

Active (F171) Type 21 frigate, 57, 88, 89
Adept SD 'Adept' class tug, 26
Alacrity (F174) Type 21 frigate, 50, 61
Albion (L14) LPD, 22, 121
Amazon (F169) Type 21 frigate, 90
Ambuscade (F172) Type 21 frigate, 46, 59
Anglesey (P277) offshore patrol vessel, 114
Antelope (F170) Type 21 frigate, 47
Appleleaf (A79) 'Leaf' class support tanker, 78
Argus (A135) aviation training ship, 10, 85, 86
Argyll (F231) Type 23 frigate, 14, 99
Ark Royal (R09) aircraft carrier, 49
Ark Royal (R07) 'Invincible' class aircraft carrier, 82, 117
Arrow (F173) Type 21 frigate, 58
Atlantic Conveyor requisitioned merchant ship, 55
Avenger (F185) Type 21 frigate, 60, 80
Battleaxe (F89) Type 22 Batch 1 frigate, 51, 92, 93
Biter (P270) 'P2000' class patrol craft, 29
Black Rover (A273) 'Rover' class small fleet tanker 110
Boxer (F92) Type 22 Batch 2 frigate, 67
Brave (F94) Type 22 Batch 2 frigate, 67
Brecon (M29) MCMV, 70, 131
Brilliant (F90) Type 22 Batch 1 frigate, 91
Broadsword (D31) 'Weapon' class destroyer, 44
Broadsword (F88) Type 22 Batch 1 frigate, 68
Bulwark (L15) LPD, 23, 122
Campbeltown (F86) Type 22 Batch 3 frigate, 71, 96
Careful SD 'Adept' class tug, 26, 36
Cawsand SD 'Storm' class tender 140
Chatham (F87) Type 22 Batch 3 frigate, 126

Cleopatra, (F28) 'Leander' class frigate, 61

Cornwall (F99) Type 22 Batch 3 frigate, 8, 70, 97

Coventry (F98) Type 22 Batch 2 frigate, 95

Danae (F47) 'Leander' class frigate, 87

Daring (D32) Type 45 destroyer, 15, 125

Devonshire WWII cruiser, 42

Diamond (D34) Type 45 destroyer, 16

Diligence (A132) fleet repair ship, 138

Dragon (D35) Type 45 destroyer, 7, 124

Dulverton (M35) MCMV, 113

Duncan (D37) Type 45 destroyer, 16

Eastbourne (F73) Type 12 frigate, 45

Echo (H87) survey vessel, 134

Edinburgh (D97) Type 42 Batch 3 destroyer, 98

Faithful SD 'Adept' class tug, 36

Fearless (L10) LPD, 106, 107

Forth (A187) submarine depot ship, 47

Fort Austin (A386) RFA, 78

Fort Grange (A385) RFA, 111

Fort Rosalie (A385) RFA, 142

Fort Victoria (A387) RFA, 117, 142

Galatea (F18) 'Leander' class frigate, 63

Gleaner (H86) survey launch, 133

Gloucester (D96) Type 42 Batch 3 destroyer, 127

Gold Rover (A271) 'Rover' class small fleet tanker 32

Grafton (F80) Type 23 frigate, 129

Guernsey (P297) offshore patrol vessel, 72

Headcorn (A1766) fleet tender 115

Hecla (A133) survey vessel, 73, 112

Hermione (F58) 'Leander' class frigate, 62

Illustrious (R06) aircraft carrier, 13, 84, 85, 119

Invincible (R05) aircraft carrier, 118

Iron Duke (F234) Type 23 frigate, 130

Kent (F78) Type 23 frigate, 21

Kinterbury (A378) RMAS armaments carrier, 81

Ledbury (M30) MCMV, 131

Lion (C34) cruiser, 43

London (F95) Type 22 Batch 2 frigate, 69

Liverpool (D92) Type 42 Batch 2 destroyer, 127

Lyme Bay (L3007) LSD, 25

Messina (L3043) LST, 48

Monmouth (F235) Type 23 frigate, 128

Mounts Bay (L3008) LSD, 25, 123

Naiad (F39) 'Leander' class frigate, 50

Norfolk (F230) Type 23 frigate, 97

Northumberland (F238) Type 23 frigate, 18, 19, 21

Nottingham (D91) Type 42 Batch 2 destroyer, 100, 101

Ocean (L12) LPH, 22, 108, 119, 120

Olmeda (A124) RFA, 78

Orangeleaf (A110) 'Leaf' class support tanker, 35, 140–141

Orwell (M2011) minesweeper, 114

Penelope (F127) 'Leander' class frigate, 62

Plymouth (F126) Type 12 'Rothesay' class frigate, 64, 65, 66

Portland (F79) Type 23 frigate, 20

Protector (A173) ice patrol/survey vessel, 30, 31

Regent (A486) RFA AEFS, 77

Roebuck (H130) survey vessel, 112

Roysterer (A361) RMAS ocean-going tug, 54

St. Albans (F83) Type 23 frigate, 20

Salisbury Type 61 frigate, 49

Saluki (A182) RMAS 'Dog' class tug, 80

Scott (H131) survey vessel, 28

Sentinel UK Border Agency cutter, 143

Severn (P282) 'River' class patrol vessel, 134

Sheffield (F96) Type 22 Batch 2 frigate, 94

Sir Galahad (L3005) LSL, 109

Sir Geraint (L3007) LSL, 76

Sir Tristram (L3505) LSL, 109

Smit Dee aircrew training vessel, 37

Somerset (F82) Type 23 frigate, 3, 17

Stubbington (M1204) 'Ton' class minesweeper, 72

Superb (S109) 'Swiftsure' class SSN, 74

Sutherland (F81) Type 23 frigate, 24

Swiftsure (S126) 'Swiftsure' class SSN, 75

Talent (S92) 'Trafalgar' class SSN, 26, 27, 104

Tartar (G43) WWII destroyer, 39

Tracker (P274) 'P2000' class patrol vessel, 137

Tyne (P281) 'River' class patrol vessel, 28

Upholder (S40) submarine, 103

Ursula (S42) submarine, 105

Valiant WWII battleship, 39

Venus (F50) Type 15 frigate, 45

Victoria SD research and support vessel, 34

Walney (M104) 'Sandown' class minehunter, 132

Wave Knight (A389) 'Wave' class large fleet tanker, 139

Wave Ruler (A390) 'Wave' class large fleet tanker, 32, 139